WILLIAM ALEXANDER ORIBELLO
SACRED MAGIC

LET THERE BE LIGHT

Published by:
INNER LIGHT PUBLICATIONS,
Box 753, New Brunswick, NJ 08903

SACRED MAGIC

Copyright 1984

Enlarged and Revised Edition

Copyright 1992

By William Alexander Oribello

ISBN#0-938294-26-1

Published by;
INNER LIGHT PUBLICATIONS
P.O. BOX 753
NEW BRUNSWICK, N.J. 08903

Free book catalog upon request.

DEDICATION

I would like to give special thanks to the wonderful people who instructed and guided me to the path of finding The Magical Temple of Light during my youth: Mr. Alexander Silverberg, Delores Brown, Professor S.D. Pickens, and others who cannot be mentioned by name for various reasons.

Current inspiration and loving support, has been given to encourage me in producing this revised edition of Sacred Magic by very special friends: Dr. Bart Mitchell, Christina Sanders, Maria Romero, Carlton Davis, Wayne Robinson, Inez Schimmelpfenning, Dorothy Calcagno, and Timothy Green Beckley.

Also, special thanks is given to my wife, Gayra, who lovingly devoted many hours in editing and typesetting this work, and to my daughter, Olivia, for giving of her personal time in assisting the proof reading of this manuscript.

All honor is offered to Divine Mind and the Ascended Masters of Wisdom for inspiring the writing of this book.

ABOUT THE AUTHOR

Since 1965, William Alexander Oribello has taught thousands of people how to improve their life in every way, through the proper application of Mystical Sciences.

During childhood, he had many experiences which guided him to first hand encounters with both Inner Plane and Living Adepts of the Secret Wisdom.

Mr. Oribello has delivered thousands of lectures, and his writings have been studied by seekers of Truth around the world.

At the present time, Mr. Oribello is accepting a limited number of students and clients, for those who are ready to enter the Path of Higher Initiation into The Divine Mysteries and The Great Work.

If, after reading this book, you feel the inner guidance for further instruction, write a letter concerning your past studies/experiences and future aspirations. Mail your letter to the author in care of the publisher, at the address below:

William Alexander Oribello
c/o INNER LIGHT PUBLICATIONS
P.O. BOX 753
NEW BRUNSWICK, N.J. 08903

INTRODUCTION

THE MISSION OF THIS BOOK

As we stand at the threshold of the 21st. century, we learn by observation that some things never change: Nearly every human being is still asking the eternal questions of, "Where did I originate? What is my purpose in life? What reality awaits me in the unknown, beyond my present life? How can I control my own life in relation to outside influences?"

Some answers to these, and other questions will be found within the pages of "Sacred Magic". One book of paper and ink cannot possibly contain all wisdom. However, such a book as this will serve as a springboard to awaken certain potent faculties, hidden within the esoteric structure of every living creature, in all time, space and dimensions.

To gain the most from this book, it is suggested that you read it casually from cover to cover. Then Read it again slowly, taking the time to practice some (or all) of the techniques, depending on your surroundings and degree of privacy.

You will notice the usage of the term "God" throughout this book. This is because most of its readers will have a traditional religious background. However, in truth, the Supreme Being is Pure Cosmic Essence-manifesting as both masculine and feminine in our highest form of comprehension - Divine Mother as well as Heavenly Father. Such is the mission of this book: To demonstrate the oneness of magic and true religion, and to use this two-fold unity as a tool to make a better person and a better world.

Many well meaning, but misinformed people associate magic with something evil or forbidden. This is because of misguided religious leaders who try to keep the masses in the grip of fear and ignorance. But as one age passes into another, we find that many people are claiming their Divine Right to decide for themselves as to what or what not to do. We are entering the long awaited Aquarian Age of Enlightenment, and find that even in this epoch of modern technology, people are seeking for the roots of an ancient "Secret Wisdom" to control their own lives, have greater well beingness, more success and prosperity. People are returning to Magic.

Several thousand years ago, one of the oldest religions in the world was about to become established, an Ancient Religion of Magic was founded, in the part of our globe later known as Persia. A man known as Zoroaster founded this religion. Later, some of the keepers of his Esoteric Teachings migrated to the continent of Africa, and were known there as "the Medianites".

In the opening chapters of the Book of Exodus, we see how Moses was tutored in the Knowledge and Wisdom of Egypt. When Moses realized he was of Hebrew Origin, he tried to free his people. He failed and was exiled from Egypt, banished to his own fate as a drifter in the desert.

Moses found his true destiny when he met Jethro, the Priest of Median (A Magi Initiate) and married his daughter. After 40 years Moses received and experienced Divine realization as recorded in the incident of "the Burning Bush". Moses was a true master of this Religion of Magic. Moses returned to Egypt and was able, with his wisdom and power, to free his people from bondage.

This Ancient Religion of Magic was not dogmatic and not one of blind faith, but one that used hidden laws of nature and believed in Divine Mind within one and all things. They believed in using these hidden laws to improve humankind as long as it was in harmony with the Divine Master Plan for the highest good of all involved.

Three Magi visited Jesus and brought him gifts of Gold (symbolic of nobility of character), Frankincense (symbolic of Divine Wisdom), and Myrrh (symbolic of personal power and self-mastery). These three Magi were called Astrologers, Kings of the East (Advanced Initiates), but most commonly were called "Wise Men". Today these three souls are now members of the Cosmic Hierarchy, also known as the Ascended Masters of the Wisdom. This Religion of Magic is seen throughout the Holy Bible.

I will demonstrate how some modern religious practices, as well as new age groups who focus on the intellectual approach, use the roots of magic in their presentations and practices.

Several Christian Churches use candles, incantations, incense, hand gestures, and other practices. Many of these practices were borrowed from the Ancient Mysteries, the Religion of Magic. Some Charismatic Christians practice clapping and raising of hands to "Praise the Lord" to the beat of Gospel Music. This is similar to how the American Indians, the Voodoo and the "Whirling Dervishes", and other cultures practice magic.

Some New Age practices such as Yogic Chanting, Aromatherapy, Rebirthing and others have their roots in ancient and modern magic. The wise ones of old have recorded the effects of certain herbal combinations, incense, oils, candles and ect. They even used an advanced form of Hypnotism in their Initiation Rites, to free the initiate of subconscious blocks, so that their lives would be transformed into one of great power. This was similar to what is now called rebirthing. The ancient Magi also taught that "he who possessed the Power of the Spoken Word" was the greatest initiate. This reminds us of modern day "Yogic Chanting" and "Affirmations" .

These examples may seem strange to you, however, when your awareness is opened it will become apparent to you. All is one and one is all. Government, religion and magic started out the same way. They were all for the good and benefit of humankind. All these things are good, essentially, it is only the misuse of these things that have given them a bad name, (including religion).

1. THE SEVEN FOLD PATH TO POWER

Before we explore the Seven Fold Path, I will reveal the great foundation for success in all types of mystic and psychic development; It is deep breathing and relaxation. This practice has been referred to as "The Silence", "The Inner Temple of Prayer" and by many other terms. It is, simply stated, going within to the very center of our being by stilling the senses and relaxing the physical body. This is the supreme method for opening our inner awareness.

THE METHOD

Sit relaxed or lie down and become as comfortable as possible. Make sure you do this at a time when you will not be disturbed. If you should fall asleep it would be perfectly alright, however, it would be better to stay awake so you may be more aware of what is taking place within you.

Take several deep breaths as follows: Inhale to the count of six, and hold the breath to the count of three. Now exhale to the count of six, and hold the breath out to the count of three. Repeat this several times and then return to normal breathing.

Now think of your feet, consciously willing that your feet become relaxed. Continue thinking of your feet until you are satisfied that they are relaxed. Now you will think of each major part of your body, one by one. You will consciously relax each area. For example, you will think of your legs up to the knees, your thighs up to the hips, your stomach and lower back, chest and upper back, hands and arms, shoulders and neck, face and head. This technique is the perfect beginning to all prayers and meditations. You must be in a state of relaxation to attain total inner awareness.

THE SEVEN FOLD PATH TO POWER

This path constitutes seven mental qualities which we develop for the purpose of opening our inner awareness to an advanced degree. They were revealed to me by a master teacher many years ago and are very powerful. They are as follows:

1. OBSERVATION
2. VISUALIZATION
3. CONCENTRATION
4. MEDITATION
5. DISCRIMINATION
6. CONTEMPLATION
7. ADORATION

We will now examine each of these seven qualities and techniques.

OBSERVATION

This means to take special notice of things which we see with our physical sight. For example, the average person looks at a long stem red rose and that's all they see. On the other hand, a person with a trained sense of observation can see how many thorns are on the stem, the stem's various shades of green, the minute shades within the color of the rose, how each petal is shaped and more.

When you develop observation you not only see an object but you will truly know it. The more you observe yourself in thinking and actions the more you will know who you really are.

HOW TO DEVELOP OBSERVATION

Practice by noticing small details about different people and objects. Become more aware of events happening around you.The most important practice is to become more aware of your mental thought processes. What thoughts are going through your mind? What messages are you receiving?

VISUALIZATION

A great form of mental magic is to visualize what you desire as already accomplished in your mind. Simply stated, visualization is forming a perfect picture of your desire. You visualize this picture until you can actually feel your desire manifested into reality.

HOW TO DEVELOP VISUALIZATION

Begin your practice of visualization by becoming totally relaxed. Then begin to form a perfect mental picture of what you wish to accomplish. Add extra details until this picture is exactly what you want. Feel the joy of receiving the answer to your prayers. Visualization is, in fact, a form of dynamic prayer. Next is the most important step in your practice. Release the picture. Don't worry about how it will come about or when. Just release it to the Universe. Stop your practice now and do something else. Forget about it until your next

session. You will find it will become
easier to obtain your desires if you do
the practices as instructed.

I would like to explain why releasing
your perfected picture is one of the most
important parts of visualization. It is
based on a sound metaphysical principle.
If you think about your desire constantly
this causes you to hold it down to this
level of limitation. You will think of so
many ways of why and how it is impossible
to obtain. However, when you release your
perfected visualization, you turn it over
to the all powerful Cosmic Mind. Your
desires may come at an unexpected time
and in an unexpected way. You should
release and trust in the all wise and
knowing "Higher Power". That Universal
Power, will then transform your perfected
picture into material opportunities. Your
response to these opportunities will
determine how quickly your desires will
be manifested

CONCENTRATION

Your practice for concentration also
includes visualization. You will begin by
visualizing and then try to generate all
of your energy into your one object of
thought. This is concentration and if you
can do this for as little as thirty
seconds you have achieved a great deal.
The mind loves to wander and flutter from
thought to thought. In true concentration
one does not force the mind to be still,
but to run through its course of thoughts
for several moments, after which it will
begin to slow down. It is when your mind
slows down that you can zero in with your
practices of concentration. When you can
master the art of concentration you will

be able to accomplish many things in your daily life as well as inner awareness.

HOW TO DEVELOP CONCENTRATION

Use this exercise to help you develop your power of concentration. See yourself in front of a blackboard with a piece of chalk in one hand and an eraser in the other. Write the letters of the alphabet, one by one, on the blackboard. Use your eraser to erase each letter before you write the next one. If your mind wanders just gently bring your attention back to what you are doing. Start by working one third or halfway through the alphabet and then increase the time span until you have used all twenty six letters. You may then begin using numbers with this same method. Begin with the number one and go through to twenty five. Extend this until you can count to one hundred.

MEDITATION

The word meditate means to think quietly or to reflect. You can see how meditation is a part of concentration, visualization and observation. Meditation is often used to replace the word prayer. In fact, it is a prayer. Here is another explanation of meditation. Meditation is to consider all you know about an object or person. You then create a void within your mind so that you can receive more impressions and information about the object of your meditation.

HOW TO DEVELOP MEDITATION

Sit down at a table with pen and paper. You will now write down the object of your meditation. List every detail about what you already know of the subject. Now write out the fact that you want to know more. Place a dark colored cloth on the table and then place your paper on top of the table in front of you. Now go into a mental state of silence by bringing deep relaxation to your physical body. (See description for this practice on page 9 and 10). Open your eyes and place your elbows on the table. Cup your hands and place them around your forehead and eyes. Do this as if you are trying to shut out any distractions. The dark cloth and the cupping of your hands help you to focus your total attention on the paper. After you have considered your subject, create a mental void by closing your eyes as though your eyelids were a wall or curtain. See this curtain come down between your perception and the object of your meditation. During the few moments following the void is when you will receive your impressions from a higher consciousness, which will inform you and guide you in reference to your object. Be patient and remember that practice makes perfection.

In order to understand how this method really works you should also understand what is known as Sympathetic Attraction. You and every other person in the cosmos are linked together mentally. This means that all minds can affect other minds. If you pick up negative energy from other minds, it is because you are allowing yourself to be negative at this time. In other words you attract other thoughts which are sympathetic to your own. The ancients embodied this concept in the axiom, "Like attracts like". By the same principle you can attract more positive inspiration from illuminated minds. It is only your lack of awareness of the Cosmic Mind which blocks your path. By constant practice you begin to break the barriers, then you develop a rapport with all other minds of power and thus become attuned to God's mind.

DISCRIMINATION

Discrimination means non-attachment and indifference. This does not imply that you should be cold or insensitive, but that you should consider the true value of things you desire and their illusions. You have to discriminate between the real and the unreal. You must know what is the most important things in your life and if they are indeed for your highest good. In other words know what your priorities are.

HOW TO DEVELOP DISCRIMINATION

Use this practice to increase you power of discrimination. Make a general list of all your present activities and desires. Then consider each one, asking yourself, "Is this matter really important in a cosmic sense?". If the inner answer is no, then mark a line through this item and try to eliminate it from your life and your consciousness. The key to this practice is to simplify your life by discarding all unimportant things.

CONTEMPLATION

Contemplation means to look at or think about something with deep thought. Look at the subject with an over all view type attitude. Information will come to you easily when you attain the contemplative state of thinking.

15

HOW TO DEVELOP CONTEMPLATION

There are many things you will want to contemplate about. Events or emotional feelings about your childhood, your young adult life, your current life and your future. This is a practice you may use for a number of reasons. It will help you to release negative feelings and be more positive. Remember you can't change past events but you can gain understanding and learn from them. Now begin this practice by sitting at a table with a lit candle in front of you. At first just sit and contemplate the candle flame and allow your mind to relax. Now you will want to focus upon your chosen subject. Visualize it embodied within the flame. If you are trying to release a negative fixation about the subject you should visualize a positive aspect replacing the negative. Contemplate on how to change it. If you are trying to gain understanding you should ask for insight of the subject. Most past experiences that are painful are from lack of understanding or lack of forgiveness. You will find many ways to use this practice to help yourself.

ADORATION

When you have developed along the path to a more advanced stage of contemplation you will begin to fall in love with the beauty of life. You will begin to see beyond the general appearance of people and things. You will then possess the ability to see the true essence of life and behold the face of God in everything and everyone. At this stage you begin to live in a state of grace. You will also find that the will of God becomes clear and great expectations of miracles flow.

Ugliness turns into beauty, sorrow turns into joy and hate turns into love. This is truly a state of knowing who you are.

HOW TO DEVELOP ADORATION

Take time to notice the things around you. Look at the beauty of nature. Gaze at the sunrise and the sunset. The birds, the flowers and most important look within your own being. Realize you are a part of the great cosmic plan. You are a most powerful being. You are learning how to become one with all there is.

As you practice the Seven-Fold Path to Power you will truly know yourself. You will discover by using these techniques that your true inner awareness will give you great peace and joy.

17

2. MAGICAL PROTECTION

As you follow the Seven-Fold Path to Power, you will come across other matters and areas of your life that will call for added information. You will need to learn more in order for you to master these matters. You are a multi-dimensional being. In this book I will give you the wisdom and insight to cover all these areas of your life. I also will give you the necessary tools to overcome the fears and complexes you have developed in this incarnation as well as past incarnations. In this chapter I will instruct you in the art of magical self-defense. You may ask why you would need self-defense in spiritual matters. It would not only be self-defense but also self-preservation.

As you know, when you start to practice these truths, your life will become more joyous and happy. People will start to be jealous of your progress. They may even ask you to help them but may not be as willing to work hard like you have. This is why you may wish to keep your work a secret. Telling people too much about your secret work can open you to receive bad luck or a curse against you. Yes, I know this may seem a little far out. You may think that being hexed or cursed is the work of an over active imagination. You may think that only a person that is unstable or wants to blame his or her troubles on someone else are the only people that would believe in such things.

Let us look at the principles involved.

18

As you have learned, you can create with the power of your mind. This also applies to people that wish you harm: Negative emotions are usually very strong and very powerful. For example, when one is angry, it seems easy to release this negativity with an outburst of angry energy. If you do not protect yourself, you can leave yourself wide open to such vibrations, both expressed and/or silent. This is why you will have to be more careful when you begin your work. Now I will give you the ways in which these harmful emotions can affect you and how you can use magical protection to help yourself.

WHAT IS A CURSE?

An enemy may wish bad luck on your life and plans. They hold negative thoughts to the effect that you will become ill, lose your mind, fail at business and personal relationships, be unhappy and a host of many other possible calamities. They can focus this energy against you a number of different ways. It may be for a number of petty reasons, such as jealousy, or not wanting you to be with someone or being a rivalry on your job. To put it simply, a curse is a negative energy. It may lodge itself in your mind forming a negative obsession, or a deeply rooted emotional problem. It could manifest in your body as an unnatural pain or condition. It can cause you to have accidents or to drop things, forget important things, lack of interest or attention about important matters, become easily upset, lose your self confidence, or hate others and a host of other negative feelings. I will now expose several ways by which an evil person may send a curse upon you.

19

INTIMIDATION

When someone constantly tries to insult
or make you look bad in front of others
it may be that the person is using this
evil technique to curse you. Such people
may do this in a joking way, but this has
a certain effect on you that makes you
feel cornered, helpless and embarrassed.
Beware of such people and separate from
them if it is possible. If you cannot,
take the person aside and tell them that
you insist they stop intimidating you. If
they refuse to stop, the only thing left
to do is to tell them off openly for
their lack of consideration. The reason
this is so important is because when a
person constantly, and deliberately
intimidates you, they are trying to break
down your mental and emotional shield.
This opens you up to their negative
forces. In order for a negative magic
spell to take effect, the victim's
confidence must be weakened in some way.

Another method of intimidation used by
evil workers, is to place a gum like
substance in the victim's path by an
unclean substance. This may be in the
form of grave yard dirt or some other
unclean matter. You may think this is
really using a wild imagination, but
believe me there are people that use
these methods and more. If you have
developed your power of observation you
will notice such things. To be informed
is to be protected. I will now explain
how this one practice can work. You pick
up the dust on your shoes by means of the
gum. This may even cause you to trip or
fall because the evil worker has placed
their negative wishes into this dust. In

20

this way the sorcerer is given an open door into your field of energy.

Another example of intimidation is the display of ill omens. The worker of evil places this ill omen in front of your door or on your property in an obvious place. It could be a dead black cat, a mouse, black roses or other ill omens.

You will need to know how the law of sympathetic magic works in order to be fully protected. Here is how this magic is used against you; Every human being radiates a magnetic energy field known as the aura. Through contact with parts of the victim's body such as nail clippings, hair, blood, saliva, or clothing the evil worker makes contact. Our emotional and mental energy, our physical vitality, our very life is contained within our auric force field. When a strand of hair, a nail clipping or ect. is separated from our body a portion of our life force remains on that part for a certain amount of time. Through such an item a spiritual worker can help you or an evil sorcerer can place a curse on you. One way the evil worker can harm you is by using a portion of your body to attach to a voodoo doll. They then place the doll in a fire, stick pins in it, or even suspend it with a string around its neck. While they are doing this they are placing their evil intent against you. This is why I mentioned earlier in this chapter; Angry negativity can be used against you whether it be expressed or silent. The above is the silent type of curse. I will now give you more insight on how highly emotional out bursts can affect you.

When someone becomes angry and blurts

out a highly emotional expression, such words become thought forms which grow stronger with time. The person to whom the words were directed may find they are under a curse which can only be broken if they overcome the trait which angered the other person. Some people are under curses which have followed them into many lives or incarnations. I will reveal how one can free themselves from curses such as these as we progress.

HOW TO PREVENT A CURSE

Try not to offend anyone if there is any way to avoid it. At times it is impossible to avoid offending someone because some people have peculiar ways. However, just to be mindful of their feelings will make it easier to have harmony.

In some cases your enemies are those who were once considered friends but a negative thing happened between you. Over the years, I have met many people who think they have many friends, only to find out in hard times that they were not as many as they thought. You may have a number of relationships that are casual and friendly, but this does not mean they are your true friend. A true friend is someone that will stand with you in all circumstances.

Friendship cannot be bought, nor can it be forced upon anyone. It is something that develops between two people who are attracted to each other by the means of one or several common interests. In order to have more harmony between you and another you should follow these most important tips.

1. Don't compromise your individuality. You are important. Do not try to change yourself in order to make someone your friend. This never works out.

2. Be considerate of others. If you are doing or saying anything which offends the other person, then stop saying or doing it. Always try to put yourself in the other person's place.

3. If others offend you. Tell them as soon as you are given the opportunity. You do not have to get angry before you tell them. If a person is really a friend they will appreciate your honesty.

4. Take time to listen. Really listen when others are talking. Many people hear but do not listen. This is one of the most common causes for misunderstandings.

5. If others become your enemy. You have to release them in love and forgiveness. One way to do this is to write a letter to the person. Express all of your hurts and resentments. Then burn the letter and say out loud, "I forgive and release you in cosmic love and light". This is a safe way to release your negative feelings toward the person. Holding on to negative feelings can harm you. You may have to do the above practice more that one time in order to receive peace.

6. Don't fight back. This puts you on their level of negativity. This will only cause you to attract more negative people and more negative situations. Remember this always, "Like attracts like".

7. Control your anger. Do not allow a

person to arouse your anger to the point
of an outburst. Just as angry negativity
can affect you, you can harm yourself by
releasing your anger in this way. I will
now share a great truth with you. It is
not what a person says to you that angers
you. It is what you think about what the
person said to you, that angers you.

PRACTICAL TECHNIQUES
FOR PERSONAL PROTECTION

An enemy can hinder your progress by
the look of envy, known as The Evil Eye.
This is an age old belief. In Italian
legends it is known as the Molochia
(pronounced Moloykee). It has also been
called the Overlooks. The concept behind
this belief is that one can place a curse
or hindrance upon another through the
gaze. It is not the actually gaze but the
thought behind the gaze that propels the
curse.

The eyes are a treasured possession, the
windows of the soul. This light reveals
the true personality. The eyes are very
powerful and through the gaze, they can
reveal the inner thoughts of a person.

Use the following method of protection
when you feel a person looking at you
with an evil gaze. Look at that person
right between their eyes. While you are
doing this try to generate love as you
say in your mind, "You cannot hurt me".
They will have to look away from you.

Here is another method of protection
against the Evil Eye. Use the thumb of
the hand that you write with, and make
the Sign of the Cross on the top of your
head. Then repeat the following words:
24

"Sanct Matheus, Sanct Marcus, Sanct Lucas Sanct Johannis". Do this practice for a total of three times. These words are pronounced as follows: The "a" in the word Sanc, is pronounced as in the word "arrow". This is the same in all four benedictions. Matheus: Math is like in the word "mathematics"; the "e" is said like an "a" as in the word "cake"; "us" is like in the word "us". Marcus: Mar is said like the "mar" in the word "market"; "cus" as in the word "custard". Lucas: Lu, the "u" sounds like the "oo" in the word "moon"; Cas is like the "cas" in the word "castle". Johannis: Jo is said like the name "Joe"; Hann is like the "hann" in the name "Hanna"; Is as in the word "pistol".

The method I will give you now is used as a protective shield. You will wear it on the left side of your body because you receive negative vibrations from this side.

You can prepare this symbol on a small piece of white paper, however, sincere practitioners choose to use parchment. They also use a quill pen and Dove's Blood Brand ink. You can obtain these items from your local occult/metaphysical shop.

Write the arrangement of letters as the diagram shown below.

```
               I.
            N.I.R.
               I.
       SANCTUS SPIRITUS
               I.
            N.I.R.
               I.
```

The letters I.N.R.I. often appear at the top of a Crucifix and represent the first letters of Hebrew words for the four elements. The four elements are air, fire, water and earth. The four arms of the cross represent the limitations imposed by the physical existence (the four elements) upon the soul of man. The words "Sanctus Spiritus" means Holy Spirit. This symbol of letters signifies that you receive power to overcome blocks through and by the Divine Spirit.

Once you have copied the symbol, you should wrap it in cloth and wear it pinned to your clothing on the left side.

Another powerful protection symbol, using words arranged in a certain order, is the Sator Square. This symbol was discovered carved on stone, written on scrolls and engraved on talismans.

Copy the words below. Again you may use a small piece of white paper but it is suggested that you use parchment, a quill pen and Dove's Blood brand ink.

```
SATOR
AREPO
TENET
OPERA
ROTAS
```

This diagram is also wrapped in cloth or put into a red cloth bag which has a drawstring at the top. These bags are also available at your local occult shop. You wear it pinned to your clothing on the left side.

The Sator Symbol has been interpreted to mean "the beginning and the end". The beginning of the Lord's Prayer has been found hidden within this powerful symbol.

The word Sator means "to sow" or to do our deeds. It is associated with the spiritual power of the Planet Saturn, the giver of discipline and karma. Therefore, you are asking for help to make your way easier, so that you can learn lessons through inner spiritual inspiration rather than by unfortunate experiences.

The word Arepo means "to plow" or reap the harvest of our deeds. Therefore, you are appealing to "the Lords of Karma", which are over your personal progress. You are asking assistance through your personal spirit guides.

The word Tenet means to "believe", or hold certain tenets of philosophical or religious belief. You are affirming your belief in a higher power to assist you in your daily life.

The word Opera means "the act" or the drama of an individual life. You are seeing that through your daily works and dramas are the lessons that can awaken you to higher knowledge.

Rotas means "the wheel" or the return of our actions to teach us lessons. You are realizing that life is a continuous wheel. By remembering our past and present experiences, both good and bad, you gain wisdom. You must do this with no resentment, pain or attachment.

The Sator Symbol has been used in a number of different ways. I have shown you a way to use it for your own personal protection and power.

A simple way to protect yourself is to use blessed salt and red pepper on your shoes. Use a new box of table salt, or sea salt if available, say a prayer over it. Be sincere and use your own words. Mix one part red pepper and three parts of the blessed salt. Put some of this on the outside back part of each shoe. You should do this before leaving your home so you can be protected in your steps each day.

PRACTICAL TECHNIQUES TO PROTECT YOUR HOME

To protect your home and keep evil away, you should put the herb, nettle, in front of every doorway inside your home.

You may also place mustard seeds on top of doorways and window sills.

Another method is by the sprinkling of blessed salt. You may use the same method to bless the salt that I gave you on this page, under Personal Protection. Sprinkle some blessed salt into all of the corners of your home. Once a month you should vacuum or sweep the salt, dispose of it and replace it with new salt.

TECHNIQUES TO PROTECT YOUR LOVED ONES

You may use this technique to protect your loved ones, including your friends, your family and your pets.

Use the practices you have learned to put yourself in a state of relaxation. You will use your power of imagination to visualize a stream of light coming from your forehead, between your eyes. Then see this light totally surrounding your loved one. Visualize the light in the form of a large bubble surrounding them. Repeat the following affirmation: "I send the light of love and peace to you. I place this circle of light around for your protection against all harm and so it is". Now release your work to the Higher Powers. You may repeat this method whenever you feel it is needed.

TECHNIQUES TO PROTECT
YOUR POSSESSIONS

You should use the bubble of light method to protect your possessions. This includes your personal possessions as well as your automobile. This can keep you protected against accidents and/or robbery.

THE ULTIMATE TECHNIQUE FOR
PROTECTION

Always remember that the greatest and most powerful form of protection comes from within you. To keep a positive mind and think only the highest thoughts of goodwill and harmony will keep you from harm. However, to stay strong mentally emotionally, and spiritually is not always possible. In our daily lifes of co-existing with others, we experience outside influences. This can put us in a weakened state. The first thing to do is to use some type of self-protection each day. The second thing you should do is to simplify your life by having positive influences around you. Try to avoid all types of negativity.

3.   THE KEY TO NATURE'S SECRETS

The information in this chapter was imparted to me by several wise ones; Holy men and women who have mastered many secrets of the universe. I have tried these things and found them to be effective in my own life.

RESTFUL SLEEP

Correct sleeping is very important to your health and well being. Before going to sleep, you should clear your mind of all negative thoughts and totally relax in the following manner: Lie down and take several deep breaths, hold the breath each time for just a moment and then exhale slowly through the nose. Relax, with each breath that you take, and think that all tension, worry and anger are leaving you. Breathe slowly now. Mentally withdraw the tension from every part of your body by thinking of your toes, your feet, your legs, and so forth. When you have reached your chest then start thinking of your hands, arms and shoulders. Then your neck, face and entire head. This is a wonderful exercise to relax the entire body.

POWER OF HERBS

Herbs have been used for many thousands of years to promote health and prolong youth. Consider the following list of herbs and their uses:

Anise gives a stimulating effect to the

mind and body. To use-inhale the aroma of Anise.

Canada Snake Root and Wood Betony taken as a tea can be of great help in cases of extreme nervousness.

Cheese plant leaves and Corn Silk tea are taken frequently to help with bladder and kidney problems.

Cloves are used for an aromatic inhaler. Take a small jar of vaseline and sprinkle it with cloves, eucalyptus and mint leaves. Mix well then apply to the tip of your finger and inhale the aroma.

Dandelion leaves are used as a remedy for low blood pressure. Drink as a tea.

Dandelion Root and Yarrow Herb are taken in the form of a tea to help keep diabetes in check.

Dandelion Root and Rhubarb Root are taken as a tea for liver conditions.

Garlic or Valerian Root tea is used to reduce High Blood Pressure.

Ginseng is the best means of prevention of illness and disease. It is wise to make sure you use the finest quality of Ginseng. The root extract is the most recommended form.

Golden Seal Herb Tea is said to cause a distaste for alcohol, therefore being helpful in overcoming alcoholism.

Lavender relieves headaches that are due to fatigue. To use-drink lavender tea.

31

Lily of the Valley and Lobelia used as a tea to improve heart conditions.

Pumpkin seed gives one vigor, virility, and regeneration. To use-eat the seeds.

Red Clover Blossom and Violet Leaf tea are used to combat cancer.

Wild Plum Bark and Lobelia Herb tea usually brings relief for people with Asthma.

A proven cure for hiccups is to apply the the following: Take some water in your mouth but do not swallow it. Next you must plug your ears with your fingers so that you cannot hear anything. Then you would swallow the water. Do this three to four times in succession. If it does not stop, repeat the procedure after five minutes.

A very effective cure for loss of voice due to a cold or strain, is to eat lemon peels. Wash a fresh lemon in warm water, remove the peel and eat it. Chew it thoroughly before swallowing.

Treatment for the common cold is to use the following remedy at the first sign of the cold. Place a teaspoon of baking soda in a glass of water and drink. Do this four times within a twenty-four hour period.

Natural vitamins can also be a great source to sustain health and youth. You can obtain natural vitamins and herbs at your local health food store. You can check the Yellow Page section of your local telephone directory for one in your area. If you find your area does not have such a store, you can obtain these herbs and vitamins through the mail. A good mail order store is Penn Herb Co.,The address is 603 North 2nd. St., Phila., PA 19123-3098.

GREAT REALIZATION

Much of humanity is in an illusion and they call this illusion reality. This is the cause for most of the suffering on this planet. One of the greatest of man's illusions is the belief that we need so many things and luxuries in order to be happy. A great adept revealed to me the four things that constitute existence of life on this planet. These four things are free. You do not buy them but you are responsible for the survival of them. They are as follows:

Air-One of the most precious things necessary to survival on this planet. Without it one cannot breathe and without breath the human physically dies. How many of us realize the importance of air? We pollute it every day with our inventions of progress(?) and it is becoming a rare thing to be able to take a breath of fresh air. We say we need more, more, more of this and more of that. We build more factories, produce more cars so they can continue to poison our precious air. What a dear price to pay for more of what we think we need.

Water-The human body is composed mostly of water. Through the spending of energy and the passing of time, the cells of our body are going through a change of dying and being replaced. If we do not take in the proper materials (and in their proper quantity) the cells are not replaced as they should be and illness may set in. Water has, like our air, also been ruined and polluted through dumping of poison waste matter from factories, and other inventions of man.

RICH SOIL-Rich Soil is a great necessity because from it we grow our food. Again, there are newer techniques of agriculture being used to grow things but somewhere down the line a compromise is being made that brings about a lack of quality. I hear people say all the time that things don't taste as good as they used to.

OIL-Last, but not least, we will consider oil. The adept told me a reason for the oil that flows in the depths of the earth. Its purpose is a simple matter of hydraulics. The layers of the earth's crust are not stationary as it appears, but they are shifting. The oil makes it all move easier. So we come to understand that oil has an overall purpose to the earth. It is not just for mans use of modern inventions and to run machinery.

Much of humanity is in an illusion. We worry more about unimportant matters, not realizing the the very foundation of life on our planet is in danger. There are some organizations trying to make people aware of this danger. They are trying to save mother earth. However, until people as a whole begin to look at others as a part of themselves and at humanity as a family, will the answers come. When we all walk in harmony hand in hand regardless of race, color, or creed will we discover the greatest secret of peace

34

and   survival, and   that   is   working
together and manifesting the word,"Love".

   Take   time each day to visualize God's
light around our planet and pray for all
the people that inhabit mother earth. Do
this before you go to sleep each night.
You will find it is worth the effort.

4. STONES, COLORS, AND CANDLES

You will find when working with Sacred
Magic some will call these practices just
superstition. Some may think you are a
little unstable and some may even think
you are evil. This stems from a lack of
understanding. I will now explain that
which is termed superstition. This will
give you a better understanding of the
principles involved in this work.

There are things we see every day that
we call reality, things believed to be
based on facts. We are considering the
difference between factual realities and
superstition. We obviously understand
factual realities but do not understand
superstition. The difference between the
two is the limit of our understanding. We
must remind ourselves that what we
believe to be reality, in some cases,
cannot be seen, felt or heard. For
example, we cannot see, hear or feel our
thoughts but we know that we think. We
know there are sounds that we cannot see,
hear, or feel such as radio/tv sound
waves. Here is another example. Before
the introduction of radio, people would
have thought it impossible. They were so
amazed. "A talking box?", I know that if
it had been discovered years earlier, the
inventor would have been condemned as a
sorcerer and would have been burned up
along with his "Magic Talking Box". This
can apply to many things today, with so
many new inventions. I just wish to open
your understanding to the possibilities

of the higher side of life.

Superstitions begin to fade as we are given the understanding behind the hidden symbolism. Superstition then becomes reality to us based on the knowledge of the laws at work in them.

MYSTIC STONES

I will now share valuable information concerning the mystic properties and use of certain stones.

LOADSTONES-It is said that to wear one of these stones on each side of your body, will balance your magnetic power. They are also used to draw out and neutralize negative conditions in healing work.

TIGER'S EYE-Use this stone to attract health, happiness and prosperity. If rubbed on the eyelids it is said to improve eyesight.

LAPIS LAZULI (AZURE)-This stone is kept for universal harmony with divine cosmic love. Used also for psychic protection.

AMETHYST-Used to bring honor and soberness of mind. It repels evil influences. When worn to bed it brings pleasant dreams and a good night's rest.

MOONSTONE-It is said to preserve youth. Used to open the faculties for enchanted memories and prophecy when placed between the eyes. Also, brings peace of mind and inner security.

CRYTALS-These valuable gems of nature are composed of the highest vibration of condensed matter, able to contain the program of creation itself from the Universal Mind. Crystals can store and channel energy. Because crystals are amplifiers for any energy programmed into them, they can be used as a tool to enchance the energy in your magical work. One may breathe their visualizations into a crystal and enhance the power of that thought. One may intone a chant into a crystal and amplify its power many times. To develop psychic powers, place on a black cloth and then place a lit candle several inches to the left of the crystal. Then you would gaze into the crystal.

COLOR MAGIC

I will now discuss colors. Following is the seven colors of the spectrum with their mystical properties explained.

1. **Red** is a stimulating color. It is connected with love, awakening, and passion. It corresponds to the element of earth.

2. **Orange** is associated with the sunset and has a healing effect on the nerves. It corresponds to the element of water.

3. **Yellow** is associated with sunlight and stimulates the emotions. it corresponds to the element of fire.

4. **Green** is associated with development and has a peaceful effect. It corresponds to the element of air.

5. **Light Blue** is a healing color. Its vibration has a calming effect. It also

indicates spirituality. It corresponds to the etheric substance.

6. Dark Blue is the color of high spiritual attainment. it corresponds to higher mental substance.

7. Violet is the color of the highest spirituality. It corresponds to the spirit made manifest.

CANDLE MAGIC

The human mind associates darkness with the unknown and with limitation. There is something about light that makes anything seem more inviting and promising to the average mind.

Since early times, man has used fire as a tool of prayer. The flame symbolized the Light of Divine Mind, giving hope and energy to the subject of meditation. Many practitioners use candles in the art of praying with fire.

In candleburning rituals, one focuses their attention on the flame as a doorway through which they communicate their desires to the higher dimensions. It is within the higher planes that the energy of the practitioner, together with the energy of intelligent forces, becomes a dynamo that manifests in this dimension as a turn of events, new opportunities, etc.

It has been a practice to use different color candles for different purposes. I will now give a list of these.

White Candles-Spiritual Communion, used

generally in prayer. It is also believed
that to burn white candles in behalf of
earthbound souls, sheds light on their
path.

Black Candles-Used to overcome crossed
conditions, absorb evil vibrations out
of, and away from the practitioner.

Blue Candles-Used for healing, peace and
psychic development.

Red Candles-Used for love attraction, and
physical vitality.

Pink Candles-For friendship and harmony
with others.

Orange Candles-Used to maintain physical
balance, sooth nervous systems and for
concentration.

Yellow Candles-Used to maintain emotional
balance and for higher intelligence.

Green Candles-For money attraction, good
fortune and for business.

Purple Candles-For spiritual attainment
and personal power.

You can obtain the different color
candles from your local occult supply
shop. However, if it is not possible to
obtain color candles, you may use a white
candle for all your needs. White reflects
all colors and is the color of purity.
You will also need a good all purpose oil
for blessing your candle. This is also
available from your local shop. The
following is how to consecrate the oil
for blessing your candles.

HOW TO CONSECRATE OIL

Olive oil or All purpose oil may be used. Place some oil in a bowl in front of you. Now take several deep breaths as follows: Inhale to the count of six, and hold the breath to the count of three. Exhale to the count of six, and hold the breath out to the count of three. Repeat this several times. As you do this, you will concentrate on the energy that you are creating to be stored in your hands. Hold both hands over the bowl of oil. Now visualize a white light coming from your hands and going into the oil. See the white light pushing out and dissolving all negativity. As you see the bowl of oil becoming one with the white light, say the following: "I bless this oil to become a Holy Anointing Oil to bless my candles." Store the oil in a clean jar until you are ready to use it.

HOW TO CLEANSE AND BLESS CANDLES

To clean your candles. First rub them completely with mineral oil then rub the wicks with water. Wipe with a clean cloth and let set a few hours.

Blessing a candle is done one of two ways. This depends on the purpose, either attracting or repelling.

If you are blessing the candle to drive away or remove a negative condition, do the following: Take some of your blessed oil on your right thumb and first two fingers. Touch the center of the candle and rub it towards the bottom of the

41

candle, one time. Take more oil on the same fingers. Touch the same center spot of the candle and rub towards the top of the candle, one time. While you do this think of the undesirable condition going away from you. Below is a diagram of how to do this.

Blessing a Candle to Repel

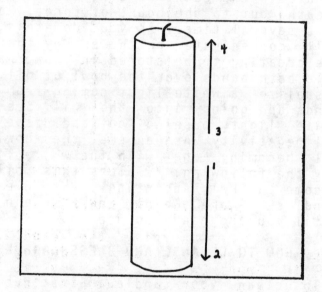

If you are blessing a candle to attract desired conditions do the following: Take some blessed oil on your right thumb and first two fingers. Touch the bottom of the candle and rub towards the center, one time. Take more oil on the same fingers and touch the top of the candle and rub towards the center, stopping at the same center spot. On the next page is a diagram to show you how to do this.

BLESSING A CANDLE TO ATTRACT

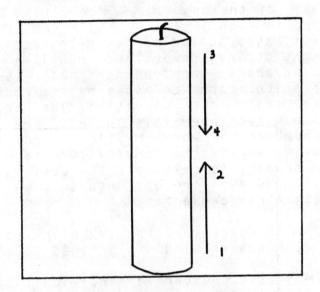

WHEN TO BURN CANDLES

If you are burning the candle for yourself you must do so during your mystic hour. To find your mystic hour, simply add all the numbers in your birthdate. If your date of birth, for example, is 12-11-1944 you would add 1+2+1+1+1+9+4+4= 23. Since your answer is not one of the two digit numbers on the clock, you will have to reduce it to a single digit, add 2+3= 5. Your mystic hour would be 5 A.M. or 5 P.M. You may burn your candle at either time or at both times. If your first addition gives you 10, 11, or 12 then that is your mystic hour. If you have any other two digit number, you will have to reduce it to a single digit. If for someone else you will use their date of birth.

5. THE NUMBER SECRET

For ages humankind has been fascinated by the obvious powers and mystical uses of numbers, each number has its own vibration. Each combination of numbers have their own vibration. The ancient philosophers knew this and used the power of numbers to work mystical practices. They also taught their students how to use numbers to calculate the best months, days, and even the best hours in which to begin a new project.

I will now reveal the symbolic meaning of each number with its alleged powers.

ONE-is the number of individuality. It represents God, the one universal mind in and around all there is. One represents the primal element, the one source of all life....The Beginning.

TWO-represents the duality within all things. It also is symbolic of the law of opposites such as heat and cold, day and night, positive and negative, ect.

THREE-is representative of the triune manifestation of Father, Son, and Holy Spirit: The trinity of time, when we consider time as past, present, and future. The three points of a triangle are symbolic of this number as time, space, and consciousness.

FOUR-is the number of a good foundation and balance. There are four corners of a house. Four seasons of the year which are

44

winter, spring, summer, and fall. There are four elements. They are earth, air, fire, and water. The four great virtues are patience, temperance, fortitude, and justice.

FIVE-has great mystic virtues for it is symbolic of uniting our duality with the power of the trinity; 2 + 3= 5. It also reveals the hint of the mystic formula for the regeneration of humankind. When we have accomplished balance and harmony between the duality of our being, natural and spiritual, we then become master of the three lower realms of existence. These levels are the physical, the emotional, and the mental. We then form the reflection or microcosm of the three-fold nature of God. There are five fingers on each hand, five toes on each foot, and five extremities of the body. The five extremities are two arms, two legs and the head.

SIX-is often referred to as the number of man, for it is written that man was created on the sixth day of creation. It is symbolic of the six pointed star known as The Star of David. The symbol of the six pointed star consists of two triangles, one pointing up (representing perfected man or the striving to perfection), and the other pointing down (representing the Divine reaching into our lives). This is the supreme accomplishment of the initiate - to unite the trinity of our being with the trinity of the Divine so that we may attain cosmic consciousness or oneness with the Universal Mind.

SEVEN-has been called the perfect or divine number. There are seven states of matter which manifest as the seven realms of existence; the seven-fold man; seven spirits of God before His throne; the book of seven seals; seven life waves; the seven stars; and seven symbolic churches of the book of Revelation; the seven energy centers of the etheric body.

EIGHT-is the number of universal harmony, for it symbolizes the axiom, "As above, So below" by its appearance of two circles, one atop the other. It has been called the number of Jesus, The Christ, and also the number of regenerated man who has attained harmony and oneness with the higher life.

NINE-is also called a perfect number because of the thirty three symbolism; Jesus is said to have lived on earth for 33 years after which he completed his mission. There are 33 degrees of study in some of the wisdom schools. The 33 must be multiplied as 3 x 3 = 9. In this arcane formula man accomplishes the perfection of his three lower bodies, the three higher bodies, and unites them with the three-fold aspect of Divinity.

TEN-is the number of completion. One is the beginning or alpha; Zero is the ending or omega. This makes ten the number of the completed work or the creation, the Kabbalistic Yod.

THE MYSTIC 9 - GOOD & EVIL

Here is some additional information concerning the number nine. It is the number of the human path of wisdom for either good or evil. For instance, in the thirteenth chapter of the Book of Revelation we are told about the Anti

Christ and the Mark of the Beast. We are
told that the Number of the Beast is
related to man and the number is 666. Now
if you add these numbers thus you have
the number 18; 6 + 6 + 6 =18. When you
add 1 + 8 you have 9. This means that
this is the evil path of wisdom or the
carnal knowledge which most humans cling
to.

In the next chapter of Revelation, we
are told of the righteous people of God
on Mount Zion. Their number is 144,000.
Again, if we add these numbers we come
out with nine, 1+4+4+0+0+0= 9. This is
symbolic of the sacred path of wisdom or
the spiritual knowledge of regenerated
man.

MAGIC IN YOUR NAME

Your name contains your own mystic
number which you can use in various ways
to help yourself. I wish to explain that
there are only nine numbers. Any number
beyond nine is just a combination of
numbers. For example 12 is a combination
of 1 and 2. In all work regarding numbers
the combination must be added together to
produce a single digit number.

Now I will show you how to receive your
mystic number from the vibration of your
name. Using the chart below you will
notice the letters of the Alphabet listed
under the numbers 1 through 9.

1	2	3	4	5	6	7	8	9
A	B	C	D	E	F	G	H	I
J	K	L	M	N	O	P	Q	R
S	T	U	V	W	X	Y	Z	

It is very simple to find your mystic

name number. I will explain by way of an example. I will use the name John Henry Smith to demonstrate. J = 1, O = 6, H = 8, N = 5. Add the numbers for the first name, John, 1 + 6 + 8 + 5= 20. Reduce 20 down to 2 (2 + 0= 2). This means that John vibrates to the number 2. Now take the name Henry. H = 8, E = 5, N = 5, R = 9, and Y = 7. Add the numbers for Henry, 8 + 5 + 5 + 9 + 7= 34. Reduce 34 down to 7, (3 + 4= 7). Henry vibrates to the number 7. Now find the numbers for Smith. S = 1, M = 4, I = 9, T = 2, and H = 8. Add the numbers for Smith, 1 + 4 + 9 + 2 + 8 = 24. Reduce 24 to 6, (2 + 4= 6). Smith vibrates to the number 6.

Now you will add the three numbers of the name together. John=2, Henry=7 and Smith=6, now you have 15, (2+7+6=15). Reduce 15 to 6, (1 + 5= 6). This persons name number is 6.

At this stage we will find the person's birth number. This is obtained by adding the day, month and year of birth. For example, let us say John Henry Smith was born on November 17th., 1934. Since it is the 11th. month, the 17th day, and year 1934, you would add like this; 1 + 1 + 1 + 7 + 1 + 9 + 3 + 4= 27. Reduce 27 to 9, (2 + 7= 9). So the birth number would be 9.

Next I will show you how to determine the number of destiny of a person. To find this you just add the name number which is 6 and the birth number which is 9,(6 + 9= 15). Reduce 15 to 6, (1+5= 6). So the number of destiny is 6.

You now have the name, birth and destiny number for our example, John

Henry Smith. If John wanted to find his
best three digit number for any purpose,
it would be 696. If he wanted a single
digit, he would just add 6+9+6=21. Reduce
21 to 3, (2+1= 3).

YOUR MAGIC HOUR

To find the best hour in which to do
anything, simply add the month, day and
year of your birthday. Reduce it to a
single digit. The birth number tells you
the best hour to perform any undertaking,
A.M. or P.M.

6. SECRETS OF GOOD FORTUNE

In this chapter I will reveal many truths about money and good fortune. You can use these truths in your daily life for more prosperity and happiness. Do the practices carefully and faithfully and you will see the results. These practices can open up new opportunities to lead you into prosperous situations.

MONEY IS GOOD

The first thing you must do is erase any idea that money is evil. Many people like to quote from the Holy Bible, the scripture which says, "The love of money is the root of all evil." After hearing this scripture many times it becomes repetitive and therefore, creates a subconscious mental block against money. I will now explain to you what this scripture really means. The evilness of money would be to place more importance on money than on anything or anyone. Also, to love money to the point of craving or lusting after it, because one lacks it. This scripture does not mean that it is evil to have or want money.

LACK IS EVIL

To crave money because of the lack of it is the root of all evil. Many people are serving time in prison because of the lack of money. The person did not realize that their own self created limitation made it so. Therefore, they came to the conclusion that the only way to obtain

50

money was to be dishonest.

Many homes have been broken because a person became so obsessed with making money that they totally lost contact with their loved ones. Money is not evil of itself. Money is good and can assist you in the comfort and pleasures of life. Think how wonderful it would be to have enough money for everything you need and also be able to help others. Worry about money causes bad nerves and even physical illness. Money can bring peace of mind which then allows you to concentrate on important spiritual matters.

POWERFUL MONEY RITUALS

I will now share some of the universal prosperity laws with you. First I will give you the following exercises to remove any negative mental blocks you may have about money. Do them daily if it is possible

Exercise #1. Relax your physical body. Use the method I gave you on page 9 and 10 of this book. When you are relaxed, visualize yourself in a room of pure white. See a small green chest (like a jewelry box) on the floor. You may see this small chest as made of jade. On the top of this chest see the words "Money is good", in solid gold letters. Now open this chest and see money springing up out of it. It is like a fountain of water but it is money. Money of all denominations. It begins to cover the floor and pile up. Use your power of visualization to bring this money to you. After this exercise get up and forget about it until the next session.

Exercise #2. King David said in Psalms 23:1, "The Lord is my shepherd, I shall not want." A wonderful thing happens when we look to God for guidance. We, then, come to a state of living where we want for nothing but that which is good for us and those around us. With this in mind take a small piece of paper and write the following words. The Lord is my shepherd, I (insert your name here) shall not want. Place the paper where you will see it the first thing each morning and the last thing each night.

Be faithful in these practices and you will soon erase all mental blocks about money.

SEVEN MONEY SECRETS

God's greatest secret of good fortune is contained in the combined realization and principles set forth in the seven money secrets listed below.

MONEY SECRET #1 - Give freely to those in need. Do not wait until you are rich, give from what you have on hand.

MONEY SECRET #2 - Do not see what you give as coming from you. See it as coming from beyond you and flowing through you. There is an important reason for this. If you see what you give as coming from you there will arise a fear that you may deplete yourself. This is because most people think of self as being limited. When you see what you give as only flowing through you and coming from a higher, unlimited power, the fear has to leave.

MONEY SECRET #3 - When you give, do not

expect anything in return. Every good deed is an investment in the universal bank which comes back to you in time, many fold.

MONEY SECRET #4 - Quit thinking negative thoughts. Work on recreating your self image. See yourself as prospering in every way.

MONEY SECRET #5 - Quit speaking negative words. Let only positive words come from your lips. if you slip, correct yourself until positive speaking becomes a habit.

MONEY SECRET #6 - Spend money for what you like to do, with what you have to work with. This makes room for self satisfaction and for more riches to come into your life.

MONEY SECRET #7 - Observe the Golden Rule which says, "Do unto others what you would have them do unto you".

These principles are the universal laws which will help change your life and draw good fortune like a magnet. Remember this scripture, "Beloved, I wish above all things that you prosper......."The Third Epistle of John, Verse 2, (The Holy Bible).

7.   THE SPOKEN WORD

Within the Holy Bible and other sacred writ are hidden words of power. These can be used as tools for manifesting certain accomplishments in your life. The Book of Psalms is one of the most popular and effective for this type of work.

Hidden in the Psalms are holy and powerful names of God and members of the Angelic Kingdom. In this chapter I will reveal the 22 words of power. These are within the 119th Psalm, which is the longest Psalm. However, for the most comprehensive study of all 150 Psalms, you should read my book, "Candle Burning Magic with the Psalms", published by Inner Light Publications. This book gives you a special formula on how to use the Divine Names of Power for each 150 Psalms.

The 22 words of power, as contained within the 119th. Psalm, concerns our present study. You should not repeat the name or the word of power out loud, only say it in your mind. Before using the divisions of the 119th. Psalm, observe the following 7 rules.

1. Light a white candle and burn some sandlewood incense. If it is possible, do not eat for a period of three hours prior to performing this exercise.

2. Enter a state of relaxation as you learned in Chapter one, page 9 and 10.

3. Try to improve your speaking habits. As you progress in this work you will develop a great power to create with your words. You do not want to create any negative conditions for yourself. Learn to speak positive about yourself, others and your situations in life.

4. Read the prescribed division of the Psalm aloud, from your heart with sincerity and emotion, followed by a prayer.

5. After reading the prescribed division of the Psalm and saying a prayer, mentally repeat the holy name of power. Do not say the holy name of power out loud.

6. While doing this part of your work, you must hold a mental picture of what you wish to accomplish.

7. After you finish your work, release it to the Higher power. The Higher power has a way of knowing just how to bring your desires into manifestation by Divine Wisdom.

22 WORDS OF POWER

You will notice that the 119th. Psalm is divided into 22 sections of 8 verses. At the head of each division is a single word. These are words of personal power and the fact of 8 verses to each division has great significance; 8 is the number of a new beginning. The word at the head of each division is one of the letters of the Hebrew Alphabet. They have been called the Alphabet of the Magi. This is because each of these words are very powerful and have a special significance.

They can lead the wise student to realms of cosmic consciousness. Following is the list of the 22 divisions with their uses according to the ancient tradition.

PSALM 119
ALEPH

VERSES 1-8 It is said that those who speak these verses in a solemn and even tone of voice can stop quivering of the limbs. Also, one will find the means to fulfill promises.

PSALM 119
BETH

VERSES 9-16 You can obtain a good memory by reading these verses on Thursday night after fasting all day.

PSALM 119
GIMEL

VERSES 17-24 It is believed these verses relieve eye pain. To be said seven times in succession.

PSALM 119
DALETH

VERSES 25-32 To be said eight times in succession every day when involved in a lawsuit. When you seek advise repeat the verses ten times.

PSALM 119
HE

VERSES 33-40 To repeat these verses will keep you from committing sins.

PSALM 119
VAU

VERSES 41-48 Speak over a glass of water for your child. It is said that the child will become obedient and will not give you problems.

PSALM 119
ZAIN

VERSES 49-56 If you have been led cunningly into a hurtful situation by a evil person/persons, repeat this eighteen times. You may then withdraw without injury to yourself.

PSALM 119
CHETH

VERSES 57-64 It is said to bring healing of pains in the upper parts of the body when repeated over wine and given to drink.

PSALM 119
TETH

VERSES 65-72 It is believed to heal pains in the kidneys when repeated reverently over the sick person.

PSALM 119
JOD

VERSES 73-80 Say this at the end of your morning prayer and your prayers will be heard and answered.

PSALM 119
CAPH

VERSES 81-88 Pray and say ten times in a

low voice to relieve sores on the right side of the nose.

PSALM 119
LAMED

VERSES 89-96 Read these verses after your evening prayer when you must appear before a judge the following day.

PSALM 119
MEM

VERSES 97-104 It is said that to pray these seven times for three days, will relieve pain in the right limbs or hands.

PSALM 119
NUN

VERSES 105-112 Said to grant you a safe and happy journey.

PSALM 119
SAMECH

VERSES 113-120 Pray these before you ask a favor of a superior.

PSALM 119
AIN

VERSES 121-128 It is said to pray these seven times for three days, will relieve pain in the left limbs or hands.

PSALM 119
PE

VERSES 129-136 It is said this cures swelling on the left side of the nose.

PSALM 119
TSADDI

VERSES 137-144 Pray these three times before a decision.

PSALM 119
KOPH

VERSES 145-152 It is believed that this cures pains in the left leg by saying over rose oil and then anointing the leg with this oil

PSALM 119
RESH

VERSES 153-160 It is believed to cure a running boil in the right ear.

PSALM 119
SCHIN

VERSES 161-168 It is said that to say these words three times over olive oil in a low prayerful voice, will relieve severe headaches when applied.

PSALM 119
TAU

VERSES 169-176 Said to relieve boil in the left ear.

In employing the 22 words of personal power, remember always that you are working with something sacred. Do not reveal to every one what you are doing. You may use this knowledge to help yourself and others, but always have any physical symptoms checked by a doctor before and after any devotional applications.

8. TRUE PSYCHIC POWERS

The word psychic means a person who is sensitive and aware of things and people without depending upon the physical senses. Mystics of all ages have taught that man possesses a sixth and seventh sense beyond the five physical senses.

All people have psychic faculties but they are undeveloped in the average person. By means of special exercises and mind expanding methods one can develop these psychic abilities.

A psychic may or may not be a spiritual person. Some groups who lack spirituality are conducting research into psychic phenomena. A spiritual person can use psychic abilities with the help of spiritual entities, depending upon the person's development.

In this chapter I explain the various psychic powers, the methods for their use and how to develop these powers.

CORRECT DEVELOPMENT

Before you do any of the practices to develop your psychic powers you should follow these guide lines. It is important to realize that these powers must be devoloped correctly and along certain lines of positive spirituality. I do not recommend anyone to take this study lightly. The horrible examples of incorrect development haunt us throughout history. Institutions for the insane are

filled with people who hear voices and
see into other dimensions. Psychopathic
killers claim that voices, or God's voice
told them to murder their victims. A
person who plays with psychic power can
fall prey to negative entities and evil
spirits who wish to possess and destroy.
Develop your powers by using the
techniques I discussed in chapter 1 and
then protect yourself by using the
methods I taught in chapter 2. Only then
should you try to develop your psychic
power.

When you feel safe in the knowledge
that you have elevated yourself into a
state of positive consciousness, only
good things will be attracted to you from
the higher levels of life. Consider the
words of Master Jesus which are
appropriate on this subject:
" And I say unto you, ask, and it shall
be given you: Seek, and ye shall find:
Knock and it shall be open. If a son
shall ask bread of any of you that is a
father, will he give him a stone? Or if
he ask a fish, will he for a fish give
him a serpent? Or if he shall ask for an
egg, will he offer him a scorpion? If ye
then, being evil, know how to give good
gifts unto your children: How much more
shall your Heavenly Father give the Holy
Spirit to them that ask Him."
St. Luke 11:9-13

THE GREAT MAGIC WORD

ABRACADABRA - This word was originally
used by the Magi to expedite development
into higher planes of consciousness. It
was worn as an amulet, engraved or
written in the form of a triangle by the
Holy Magi. Its numerical values are 22

for the path which attains to the Tree of
Life; Number 12, which means governmental
perfection, relating to the development
of character in harmony with the Twelve
Tribes of Israel, the Twelve Apostles of
Jesus and the Twelve Gates of the New
Jerusalem. Number 3 which is symbolic of
the Holy Trinity. It is written as shown
below.

```
        A
       A B
      A B R
     A B R A
    A B R A C
   A B R A C A
  A B R A C A D
 A B R A C A D A
A B R A C A D A B
A B R A C A D A B R
A B R A C A D A B R A
```

To develop psychic abilities do the
following. You may copy this magical word
on a small piece of white paper. Some
people prefer to use parchment, a quill
pen and Dove's Blood Brand Ink. This is
available through occult shops, locally
or through the mail. After you have
copied the word you should place it under
a crystal ball. If you do not have a
crystal ball you may use a clear glass
bowl filled with water. Place a black
cloth on a table. Place the magical word
under your crystal ball or glass bowl.
Light a candle and place it to your left.
Gaze at the magical word under the bowl
or crystal ball. Do this for as long a
time as you feel comfortable.

PSYCHIC SIGHT

CLAIRVOYANCE - This means "clear-seeing",

and manifests in two ways: The first is to see things, around yourself or another person, that others cannot see. It may appear that you see invisible entitles, auras, other dimensions, etc., with your physical eyes. But, actually, you are seeing these things with your "third eye" or intuitive sixth sense. The second way that this ability manifests is to know, sense or perceive by intuition, that an invisible someone or array of impressions are coming into your range of clairvoyant ability. Most psychics use this second type of clairvoyance; when they say that they see something about the person, what most of them really mean is that they sense it at an intuitive level.

HOW TO DEVELOP CLAIRVOYANCE

Light a candle, set it on a table, turn all other lights off and seat yourself in front of the candle. Just gaze at the candle for several moments. Mentally desire to see the magnetic field around the candle flame. Continue wanting to see the finer vibrations of color and symbolic images around the flame, while doing this also think of the spot between your eyebrows. This shifting of your consciousness back and forth, between wanting to see the magnetic field of the flame and thinking of the spot between your eyebrows, will help you to see with clairvoyant vision. Anytime you wish to see the colorful magnetic field around a person, do this practice. Continue this practice once or twice weekly until, and after you get results.

PSYCHIC HEARING

CLAIRAUDIENCE - This word means "clear

hearing", and also manifests in two ways: The first is where the mystic seems to actually be hearing words from an invisible person, or a conversation taking place in another dimension. They may also hear words that were spoken by or to the person for whom they are giving a reading. Actually, they are not hearing with the physical sense of hearing; they only seem to hear in that way. It is also with their sixth sense that they are able to hear. The second way that one experiences clairaudience ability is when the words come to them in "a strong thought". In other words, the message makes itself known in a series of words, seeming to saturate our consciousness. When this happens, we know somehow that it is not our thoughts, but a message from the invisible realms.

HOW TO DEVELOP CAIRAUDIENCE

Sit quietly in a room with soft lights. Relax your physical body as taught to you in chapter 1. The room should be very quiet, at an hour when there will be a minimum of outside noises. Sit for several moments listening to the silence. After awhile, direct your thinking inwardly to the sound of silence and peace. In a short time you may begin to hear what sounds like music or bells. Keep thinking upon these sounds, desiring that you receive a message. When your session is complete, write down any impressions you received. In the future, you may tune in to the inner sound while in another person's presence, to see what you can pick up in their behalf. Do this private exercise once or twice weekly.

BIBLICAL EXAMPLES OF
THE POWERS OF CLAIRAUDIENCE / CLAIRVOYANCE

"And he fell to the earth, and heard a voice.....And the men which journeyed with him stood speechless, hearing a voice, but seeing no man"... Acts 9:4-7

"And, behold, there appeared unto them Moses and Elias talking with him"...
Matthew 17:3

"Before Phillip called thee, when thou wast under the fig tree, I saw thee"..
John 1:48

"And there came an Angel of the Lord... And the angel appeared to him and said.."
Judges 6:11-12

PSYCHIC FEELING

PSYCHOMETRY-This means "clear-feeling". In this ability, the mystic holds an object in their left hand, and picks up vibrations about the owner of the object. This is possible because we leave a magnetic record of our feelings, thoughts and personality on anything we use or own.

HOW TO DEVELOP PSYCHOMETRY

Ask the assistance of a friend for practicing this ability. Have them give you an object to hold in your left hand. They should be familiar with some of the history of the object, but it should be something of which you know nothing about. As you hold the object, relax in the manner already taught to you. Then mentally ask to know something about the
65

object's past, as well as its owner. As you receive intuitive impressions, relate them to the person. Do not stop and ask if you are correct. Let the information flow until you know that you are finished.

Another method to develop psychometry is to have someone place a few pieces of spice or dry food in an envelope without your knowledge of what it is. Hold the envelope and desire to actually taste or smell what is in it. The first mental impression is usually the correct one. Remember, practice makes perfect. Do not be discouraged if you do not always obtain accurate results.

You may also practice your ability when you receive mail. Hold the letter in your hand for a few moments to see if you can pick up an indication of what's written in the letter.

MEDIUMSHIP

Spirit Communication- This is the ability of establishing a link of communication between the spirits of the departed and the living.

There seems to be conviction among most modern day christians that it is wrong to communicate with the dead. However, there is a great misunderstanding of terms in regards to this subject.

BIBLICAL PROOF OF SPIRIT COMMUNICATION

The conviction of the dogmatists seem to be founded upon a scripture found in the Old Testament of the Holy Bible. It

66

is, "Why, consult the dead on behalf of
the living?", Isaiah 8:19. I will now
attempt to explain. To most people the
word "dead" means one of two things,
depending upon their religious belief.
The first is that it means, the ceasing
of life, totally and finally. The second
is that it means the spirit of man being
separated from the body. In the spiritual
sense the word "dead" means more. The
Holy Scriptures refer to the word "dead"
as the unregenerated, or sinners. Study
the following scriptures.

"And you hath He quickened, who were dead
in trespasses and sins".. Ephesians 2:1

"Even when we were dead in sins".........
Ephesians 2:5

"And you, being dead in your sins".......
Colossians 2:13

"But she that liveth in pleasure is dead
while she yet liveth"... I Timothy 5:6

"And another of his disciples said unto
him, Lord, suffer me first to go and bury
my father. But Jesus said unto him,
follow me; and let the dead bury their
dead"...... St. Matthew 8:21-22

We see by these scriptures that they
who were unregenerated, or walking in
spiritual darkness, were considered dead
even though they were physically alive.
Therefore, it is not wrong to communicate
with spirits. It is just wrong if you
attempt to communicate with spirits of a
low order of consciousness or the
spiritually dead. This is because low
order spirits will lead you away from the

path of the true and living God. They want you to join them in their sufferings of walking in a state of Hell. They seek to confuse, trick, possess, and destroy. This is why it is so important to raise your consciousness into higher planes and be well protected before attempting contact with the spirits. You will then know the differences between the grades and motives of spirits who attempt to communicate with you. Remember the following scripture.

"Beloved, believe not every spirit, but try the spirits whether they are of God: Because many false prophets, (False Mediums), are gone out into the world..."
I John 4:1

THREE TYPES OF MEDIUMS

A medium is a person who is a channel for spirit entities to communicate with the physically alive.The three types of mediums are:

1. Mental Mediums-This is a person who receives mental impressions and messages from Spirits, Master Teachers and Angels. They communicate this information to their clients.

2. Trance Mediums-This is a person who goes into a trance so that the spirits speak through them.

3. Manifestation Mediums-This is one who is able to cause physical manifestations to prove the presence of the spirit, even producing a materialization of the spirit.

A person may possess one, two or all three of the mediumistic abilities to a certain degree.

BIBLICAL EXAMPLES OF MEDIUMSHIP

Mediumship is recorded in the Holy Bible as being demonstrated by various prophets. The word Prophet may be considered synonymous with the word Medium.

Spirit Writing-This is an ability in which someone may write a message or even a book, under the control of a spirit. King David gave his son, Solomon, a diagram from which to build the Lord's Temple. He said it came to him in writing as the hand of the Lord was upon him.
I Chronicles 28:19

The Trance-The trance state has many scriptural examples. They are:

"He hath said, which heard the words of God, which saw the vision of the Almighty, falling into a trance......"
Numbers 24:4

"....Peter went upon the housetop to pray ....He fell into a trance and saw Heaven opened....." Acts 10:9-11

"And it came to pass, that, even while I prayed in the temple, I was in a trance.."
Acts 22:17

"And I knew such a man, whether in the body, or out of the body, I cannot tell: God knoweth; how that he was caught up into paradise, and heard unspeakable words...." II Corinthians 12:3,4

69

Materialization- Apportation is our next mediumistic ability under consideration. An apport is an object, animal, or human which has been dematerialized from one location (so as to give the appearance of vanishing), and the elements rematerialized in another location as if to appear out of thin air. This is accomplished by the applied will power of a living Magi or by a person with the aid of a powerful spirit. See the following Biblical example;

"..And when they were come up out of the water, the Spirit of the Lord caught away Philip, and the Eunuch saw him no more.. but Philip was found at Azotus."

Acts 8:39,40

Levitation-At times an apport is not dematerialized but rises and floats to another location. This falls under the classification of levitation. Many Yogis, as well as Western Mystics were said to rise above the ground while sitting, standing or walking in a state of great spiritual devotion. It is recorded that Jesus walked on water.

"And when they saw him walking upon the sea, they supposed it had been a spirit.. ..."

St. Mark 6:49

"But as one was felling a beam, the ax head fell into the water: And he cried, and said, Alas, Master! For it was borrowed. And the man of God said, Where fell it? And he shewed him the place. And He (the man of God) cut down a stick, and

70

cast it thither; and the iron did swim.."
                              II Kings 6:5,6

"Jesus said, "The works that I do shall
he (who believes in me) do also."
                              St. John 14:12

Inspired Speaking- Speaking in a
foreign language: A person may, under the
influence of Holy Spirit Guides, speak in
a language that they have not learned
consciously. This would be for the
benefit of the hearer who did understand
the language, and show proof of a genuine
spirit manifestation.

Speaking unknown languages is another
mediumistic ability, also called
"Speaking in Unknown Tongues". The
scriptural examples are found in Acts,
Chapter 2 and also in I Corinthians
14:27-32.

HOW TO DEVELOP MEDIUMSHIP

First, and MOST IMPORTANT, use the
protection techniques I gave in chapter
2, before any attempt to make contact
with the Spirit World. The reason for
this, is that there are many spirits who
are earthbound, and love to play tricks
on people. You must be sure that you are
communicating with highly evolved
spirits, who would not ask you to do
anything against your highest good, or
that of others. The Holy Spirits always
advise one to participate in wholesome
things that will benefit humankind,
beginning with the medium and anyone
depending upon them.

TELEPATHY

Thought transference or mental telepathy has been a subject of psychic development for many generations. The idea is that two persons may communicate mentally within the same room or at a distance. It also means that one may send a thought to another. It is important to realize that for a person to receive a thought sent by another, it is necessary for the receiver to be in a passive state of mind. To send a thought, form a mental picture of the person you wish to contact. Before you do this, however, it is best to go into a state of relaxation. After you visualize the person, tell them your message, mentally or out loud. Then forget it until the next time. You may have to try more than once; remember, they must be in a passive state of mind to receive your message.

9. MAKE A MAGIC MIRROR

In this chapter I will share some valuable information concerning the mystic use of mirrors. You may use any mirror if it is prepared according to my instructions. You will need, as part of your preparation, the following items; blessed olive oil, a white candle, and a bowl in which you will place consecrated water. Bless the oil by the instructions on page 41. Prepare the white candle to attract, by the instructions on page 43.

WHY USE A MIRROR?

THE PURPOSE-You may accomplish the following things by using the magic mirror: Influence yourself to change habits; Communicate with the subconscious and superconscious minds; Develop spiritual sight; Ask questions of higher intelligence; Meditate; See past lives and much more.

WHEN TO USE A MIRROR

The Time-The best time of the month to do this is the first seven days before the full moon. Do not use the mirror during the full moon, only during the seven days before the full moon. Check your calendar or almanac for this schedule of the moon. The best time of the day to do this is at night between the hours of twelve midnight and four A.M. The vibrations of the earth are of a certain stillness during these hours. The solitude will help you be more receptive to spiritual impressions. You should be quiet and alone so you will not be distracted.

THE FIRST STEP

The Preparation-Boil Some water. After it has started to boil repeat the Twenty Third Psalm from the Holy Bible over the water. Allow the water to cool. Using a clean cloth or paper towel, apply the water to the mirror, covering all areas of the mirror with it.

After the water has dried on the mirror, take some blessed olive oil on the first or second finger of your right hand.Apply the oil on the center of the mirror, then smear it from the center in a line straight down, then from the center straight up. You will then smear it from the center in a line to your left and finally from the center in a line to your right. This forms a cross. See diagram below.

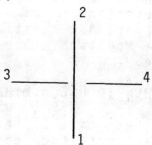

Allow this to dry. Then wash the mirror with soap and water. This preparation should be done when you are alone during the hours already mentioned and during the seven days before the full moon. You should save the water in a jar, as this is consecrated water and will be used in the work of this lesson.

THE SECOND STEP

The final preparation-When you are ready for your work, do the following things. First, draw the diagram below on your mirror. You can use a felt tip marker, as this should wipe off easily. Mark the G in the upper left hand corner.

G	I	L	I	O	N	I	N
I
L
I
O
N
I
N

After you draw the squares and letters on the mirror, place a bowl of the consecrated water between where you will sit and the mirror. Place the candle to your right.

THE THIRD STEP

When you have made all preparations and are ready to begin, bathe yourself and relax mentally by meditation on the positive results you wish to obtain. Try to keep yourself from getting upset during the day of your work.

THE RITUAL

Now you are ready to begin. First, light the candle. Then repeat the Lord's Prayer. Be sure all lights are out except the light of the candle. Gaze into the mirror looking into the eyes of your reflected image. After several minutes, speak out loud in a soft but firm voice, your reason for doing this work. For example, if you wish to change unwanted habits, you must clearly state that which you wish to stop doing and that which you desire to replace it. A very good way to change is to address your subconscious mind, asking it to reject the unwanted trait from now on and to accept that which is constructive and good. You would then request that your superconscious mind guide you into the help that you need. It is very wise and knows how to help you.

You may ask questions of higher intelligence, such as Master Teachers, Angels, Saints and Spirit Guides. It may be that you will see a vision as you gaze into the mirror or the answer may come to you in a flash of intuition. The answer may come as a dream later that night. Do not try to predetermine how the answer will come. Be open to the best way for you to receive the answer according to God's wisdom.

Gazing at your image and visualizing rays of light coming from the eyes and going into the eyes of your image, will develop a keener spiritual sight.

TAKING CARE OF YOUR MIRROR

If you wish, you can buy a mirror just for this purpose so you do not have to prepare it every time. In this case you can paint the diagram on it instead of using the felt pen. However, you must keep it wrapped in a violet colored cloth when not in use. It would be good to wash it with the consecrated water and apply the oil, as the instructions I have already given you, every ninety days.

After each session throw the water in the bowl away. Also, keep a pad and pen next to your bed so that you may write down any dreams or experience you have during the night. Much information is lost because we fail to write it down during the moment that we awake. If we go back to sleep and wake up later, we will forget much. Be consistent in your work and you will be rewarded from the higher planes of being.

10. TALISMANIC MAGIC

Mystic Seals are legendary talismans, said to contain special vibrations for specific purposes. It is believed that certain words and designs have virtues sealed within them. According to the Inner Teachings, powerful spirits revealed the designs of certain seals to the Magi, Prophets and Adepts.

Some of the legendary seals contain hidden names of the God-Power. Others contain the names of angels or specific forces of nature.

The designs on mystic seals can awaken special powers within the human mind, so that the practitioner can release the energy to the Higher Power. The Higher Power receives this energy and sends it back into our world in the form of favorable circumstances that enhance success.

In addition to the revelation given to the Wise Ones about these things, there is the great power of belief from the minds of multiplied thousands of people, who have used these seals for ages.

Talismanic Magic is one of the easiest forms of Inner Pathworking, because it is a quiet practice. One may not have the privacy for elaborate candleburning, or other rituals, but working with talismans affords you a private means of magical work.

FIVE POWERFUL TALISMANS
OF THE SACRED MAGIC

The talismans in this book may be cut out and used as instructed, however, you may wish to order a set separately. You can receive a set by writing to the publisher, Inner Light Publications, and requesting information about them.

The first four talismans are said to originate with King Solomon. The fifth is a miniature replica of the Staff of Moses. Cut out each talisman and hold them between the palms of your hand, one at a time. While you are holding the talisman in your hand say the following words:
"Blessed Be; may the Cosmic unity blend with my High Self and bring forth all my desires through this symbol of power. So mote it be."

Following is a list of the enclosed talismans with their alleged mystic virtues. You may choose to seal your talismans in plastic to preserve them.

#1 The Seal of Protection

79

CUT OUT THE TALISMAN ON THE OTHER SIDE OF THIS PAGE.

#1 The Seal of Protection

The Seal of Protection talisman is to be worn on the left side of the body.

#1 PROTECTION
Write your name here

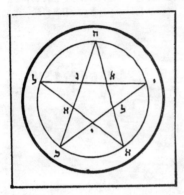

#2 The Seal of Magnetic Power

The Seal of Magnetic Power is believed to help one to become stronger and more magical. It is to be worn on the right side of the body.

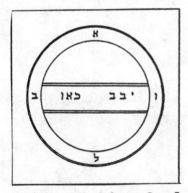

#3 The Wishing Seal

The Wishing Seal is to be placed between your palms when you are praying for a wish to be granted. It is believed that all wishes, not in violation of cosmic law, will be granted.

CUT OUT THE TALISMANS ON THE OTHER SIDE
OF THIS PAGE.

#2 MAGNETISM
Write Your Name Here

#3 WISHING
Write Your Name Here

#4 The Seal of Rest

The Seal of Rest. It is said that this sacred talisman should be kept under your pillow for a restful sleep and to help obtain more significant dreams.

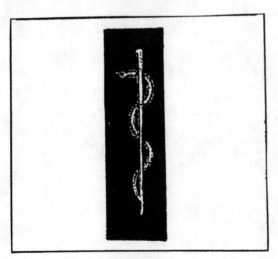

#5 The Seal of the Staff of Moses

The Staff of Moses Seal is to be held in your right hand when doing any work described in this book.

CUT OUT THE TALISMANS ON THE OTHER SIDE
OF THIS PAGE.

#4 RESTFUL SLEEP
Write Your Name Here

#5 STAFF OF MOSES
Write Your Name Here

THE HAND OF GLORY

This is the complete illustrated version of the famous Hand of Glory. It is also called Hand of the Mysteries. For many centuries mystics believed that to have even a picture of this powerful symbol in their home would protect their dwelling from all evil works, of any secret enemy or spirit who would come into the their home. However, there was a secret ritual which activated the power of the hand. I now share that ritual with you. Keep the following instructions secret - they are for you and you alone.

During the seventh day before the Full Moon you are to take a handful of salt in your right hand. Hold it tightly so that your vibrations will impregnate the salt. As you do this, repeat the 91st. Psalm. After each verse you direct your eyes away from the Bible and look at the picture for a few moments. Then continue by reading the next verse until you have read all sixteen verses and directed your gaze to the hand sixteen times. Then you are to sprinkle the salt all over the picture. After you do this set a candle holder containing a white or purple candle which you have blessed to attract, (See page 43). Place the candle on the center of the picture and burn it for a few moments each night until the first night of the Full Moon. The next and final step is to hide the picture in your home. You may place it on a table under a covering, or place it behind another picture in a frame. See page 89.

The symbolism in the picture is very

significant: At the bottom right is a sunrise, this is symbolic of our efforts or action coming forth from the right side. At the bottom left is the moon and star against the evening sky. This is symbolic of our passive state on the left side from which we receive vibrations. In the center of the hand is The Pentagram or Magical Star with a Cross at its core. This means that we are to develop The Sacred Magical Power along lines of pure spirituality. Above the five fingers are the following symbols: The Crown with a Cross, which means reward through work and perseverance. The Six-Pointed Star, symbolic of blending human will with Divine Will. The flame, which stands for the zeal and force of The Holy Spirit. The Fish, that tells us that we are to search for the Inner Self. And The Key, which reveals the clue to understanding the mysteries are in small things. It also represents The Master Key to all things.

There are four elements of the physical world, and a fifth element of higher energy. We will not go into an expanded study of the elements but you should know the relationship between the five fingers and the five elements. I will also give you the explanation of how these elements relate to our feelings and desires.

The thumb relates to the element of earth and corresponds to material matters and grounding. The first finger relates to the element of air and corresponds to mental matters. The second finger relates to the element of fire and corresponds to emotional matters. The third finger relates to the element of water and is in correspondence with higher expression of thought and emotions. The little finger relates to the fifth element of Spirit. Spirit is present in all space and time, for without it, nothing else could exist. The correspondence for Spirit is the inspiration of the Highest Order. This is The Master Key to self and Divine realization.

After following all instructions for consecrating the Hand of Glory, dispose of anything left of the candle and salt. You may do this in any way that you see fit. Some people choose to dispose of the items by burying them. Others dispose of the items by putting them in the trash. In any case these items have served their purpose, and therefore it is up to you.

Following are some Biblical examples of the power of the hand, human and Divine.

"I (the Divine Spirit) will cover thee with my hand.........."
                    Exodus 33:22

"And Jonathan ...... strengthened his hand in God (The Divine Power)".
                    I Samuel 23:16

"......there arises a little cloud (vision) out of the sea, like a man's hand......."
                    I Kings 18:44

"He that has clean hands, can reach the mountain (The High Order Of Divine Realization) ....."
                    Psalm 24:4

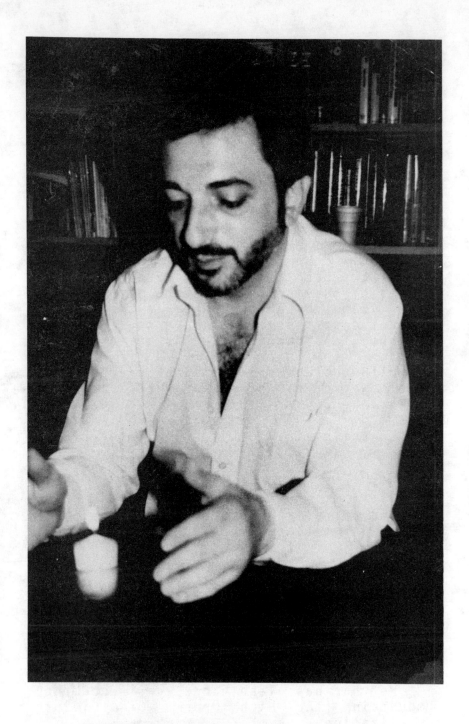

William Oribello burns candles for good luck, to celebrate release of revised edition of *Sacred Magic*.

THE HAND OF GLORY

PS. 91

.·. Blessed ·. Be ·.

CUT OUT THE TALISMAN ON THE OTHER SIDE
OF THIS PAGE.

.

Write Your Name Here

11. CHANGE YOUR LIFE NOW

In closing, I will share several practices which you may perform daily. One of the most important things to remember is this: ALWAYS PERFORM THE RELAXATION TECHNIQUE GIVEN IN CHAPTER ONE, BEFORE PERFORMING ANY OF THE FOLLOWING EXERCISES, AS THIS WILL BRING THE BEST RESULTS.

THE DAILY PRAYER

Shortly after waking up, the following prayer should be repeated softly, but with feeling and sincerity;

"Universal Mind, fill my day with Divine Cosmic Love and Harmony. Give me the guidance, courage and wisdom to face and successfully deal with the events of this day, for the highest good of myself and all others whose lives touch mine. Protect me from all danger, seen and unseen. Thank you. It is done."

NIGHTLY PRAYER

Before going to sleep, repeat the following prayer (you may say this mentally if you wish):

"Universal Mind, protect, teach and heal me as I sleep. If I have violated any universal laws this day, either by commission or omission, please forgive me. Thank you. It is done."

MAGNETIC BREATHING

This exercise is, for all practical purposes, your "Daily Bread" to empower every level of your being. It is a way of accumulating and storing what was termed "The Secret Force" and "Magnetism" by my early teachers. This force is the very essence of Universal Life and has been known by other terms, Such as "Prana", "Odic Force", "Vital Life Force", and ect. It does not matter which term is used, the Force is one.

You can use this Force as a conductor for healing, the will to break bad habits, have more magnetism in your personality, and to generally charge all your magical operations with more power. I will give you two versions of this exercise: The first is simple and quick. The second is more involved and takes more time, but you should avail yourself of the second version whenever you possibly can.

THE FIRST VERSION

The first version of the magnetic breath is as follows: Sit or stand facing the East. Take several deep breaths, and as you do so, imagine that an egg-shaped cloud of white mist has gathered around you. Now inhale deeply, only this time, imagine that you are inhaling this mist through every pore of your skin, all over your physical body. Will that this energy be stored with your physical, emotional, and mental levels of your being. Because you have, by your God Given ability of creative imagination,

92

attracted such a Force, your spiritual
self will also be enhanced.

Continue taking this Cosmic Energy into
you each time you inhale; each time you
exhale, imagine that you are letting go
of all things that hinder you, releasing
them into the transforming power of God's
Light. Do this practice for as long or
short of a time as you desire. Be sure to
take all of the mist that you mentally
attracted into your being.

THE SECOND VERSION

The second version of the magnetic
breath requires that you stand, face the
east and stretch out your arms from side
to side, forming a human cross image. Now
as you inhale deeply, imagine that you
are drawing the power of the air element
into your being, through the pores of
your skin. As you exhale, you are letting
go of all things that hinder you.

Now turn to the south, with your arms
still outstretched. Inhale while you
imagine that you are drawing the power of
the fire element into your being, through
the pores of your skin. As you exhale,
you are letting go of all things that
hinder you.

Now turn to the west, with your arms
still outstretched. Inhale while you
imagine that you are drawing the power of
the water element into your being,
through the pores of your skin. As you
exhale, you are letting go of all things
that hinder you.

Finally, turn to the north, with your
arms still outstretched. Inhale while you

imagine that you are drawing the power of the earth element into your being, through the pores of your skin. As you exhale, you are letting go of all things that hinder you.

In closing this second version of the Magnetic Breath, turn back to the east. Inhale deeply and exhale strongly, positioning your lips as though you are whistling, making a sound like a strong wind blowing through the trees.

MASTERY OF THOUGHT

By thinking, we create our everyday realities as well as our destinies. It is imperative that you become a "watcher", to guard against the negative thoughts that cross your mind.

Each time a negative thought comes into you mind, see a fire arise and burn up the negative thought. Then, instantly replace it with a positive thought, totally opposite of the negative. In doing this you will be able to discipline your mind.

MASTERY OF THE SPOKEN WORD

"In the beginning was the word....And the word was God"
St. John 1:1

As one advances in any type of magical training, they will realize that they are becoming a god, able to speak things into existence by the force of their will power. Therefore, it is important that if we say anything negative about ourselves, other people and objects, that we instantly contradict ourselves out loud by saying the opposite. In Italian Mystical Folklore, people use the term "God Forbid" when they speak of anything negative that could happen.

THERE'S MORE

If you decide to go no further than this book, then you possess a valuable tool, which if applied properly, can set you on the path towards finding a true teacher. Remember the ancient axiom: "When the pupil is ready, the teacher appears." However, if you feel guided to write me for information regarding further training, you may do so at the address below.

And now, dear friend, may the Eternal Light of Universal Mind guide you in the right direction, and crown all of your efforts with abundant success.

William Alexander Oribello
c/o INNER LIGHT PUBLICATIONS
P.O. BOX 753
NEW BRUNSWICK, N.J. 08903

CREATE LIFE'S GREATEST BLESSINGS BY COMBINING THE POWER OF THE HOLY PSALMS WITH THE MAGIC OF BURNING DIFFERENT COLORED CANDLES

BY THE SAME AUTHOR. . .

CANDLE BURNING

MAGIC

WITH

THE PSALMS

Order from: INNER LIGHT PUBLICATIONS
Dept. OL, Box 753
New Brunswick, NJ 08903

.$10.00

William Alexander Oribello